WI

New Community

KNOWING. LOVING. SERVING. CELEBRATING.

Laws That Liberate

THE TEN COMMANDMENTS

ZONDERVAN®

WILLOW
Willow Creek Resources

ZONDERVAN.com/
AUTHOR**TRACKER**
follow your favorite authors

ZONDERVAN

Laws That Liberate: The Ten Commandments
Copyright © 2009 by Willow Creek Association

ISBN 978-0-310-28062-0

Interior design by Sherri Hoffman

Printed in the United States of America

09 10 11 12 13 14 15 • 21 20 19 18 17 16 15 14 13 12 11 10 9 8 7 6 5 4 3 2 1

CONTENTS

God has created us for community. This need is built into the very fiber of our being, the DNA of our spirit. As Christians, our deepest desire is to see the truth of God's Word as it influences our relationships with others. We long for a dynamic encounter with God's Word, intimate closeness with his people, and radical transformation of our lives. But how can we accomplish those three difficult tasks?

The New Community Bible Study Series creates a place for all of this to happen. In-depth Bible study, community-building opportunities, and life-changing applications are all built into every session of this small group study guide.

How to Build Community

How do we build a strong, healthy Christian community? The whole concept for this study grows out of a fundamental understanding of Christian community that is dynamic and transformational. We believe that Christians don't simply gather to exchange doctrinal affirmations. Rather, believers are called by God to get into each other's lives. We are family, for better or for worse, and we need to connect with each other.

Community is not built through sitting in the same building and singing the same songs. It is forged in the fires of life. When we know each other deeply—the good, the bad, and the ugly—community is experienced. Community grows when we learn to rejoice with one another, celebrating life. Roots grow deep when we know we are loved by others and are free to extend love to them as well. Finally, community deepens and is built when we commit to serve each other and let others serve us. This process of doing ministry and humbly receiving the ministry of others is critical for healthy community life.

Build Community Through Knowing and Being Known

We all long to know others deeply and to be fully known by them. Although we might run from this level of intimacy at times, we all want to have people in our lives who trust us enough to disclose the deep and tender parts of themselves. In turn, we want to reveal some of our feelings, expressing them freely to people we trust.

The first section of each of these six studies creates a place for deep knowing and being known. Through serious reflection on the truth of Scripture, you will be invited to communicate parts of your heart and life with your small group members. You might even discover yourself opening parts of your heart that you have thus far kept hidden. The Bible study and discussion questions do not encourage surface conversation. The only way to go deep in knowing others and being known by them is to dig deep, and this takes work. Knowing others also takes trust—that you will honor each other and respect each other's confidences.

Build Community Through Celebrating and Being Celebrated

If you have not had a good blush recently, read a short book in the Bible called Song of Songs. It's a record of a bride and groom writing poetic and romantic love letters to each other. They are freely celebrating every conceivable aspect of each other's personality, character, and physical appearance. At one point the groom says, "You have made my heart beat fast with a single glance from your eyes." Song of Songs is a reckless celebration of life, love, and all that is good.

We need to recapture the joy and freedom of celebration. In every session of this study, your group will commit to celebrate together. Although there are many ways to express joy, we will let our expression of celebration come through prayer. In each session you will take time to come before the God of joy and celebrate who he is and what he is doing. You will also have opportunity to celebrate what God is doing in your life and the lives of those who are a part of your small group. You will become a community of affirmation, celebration, and joy through your prayer time together.

You will need to be sensitive during this time of prayer together. Not everyone feels comfortable praying with a group of people. Be aware that each person is starting at a different place in their freedom to pray in a group, so be patient. Seek to promote a warm and welcoming atmosphere where each person can stretch a little and learn what it means to be a community that celebrates with God in the center.

Build Community Through Loving and Being Loved

Unless we are exchanging deeply committed levels of love with a few people, we will die slowly on the inside. This is precisely why so many people feel almost nothing at all. If we don't learn to exchange love with family and friends, we will eventually grow numb and no longer believe love is even a possibility. This is not God's plan. He hungers for us to be loved and to give love to others. As a matter of fact, he wants this for us even more than we want it for ourselves.

Every session in this study will address the area of loving and being loved. You will be challenged, in your personal life and as a small group, to be intentional and consistent about building loving relationships. You will get practical tools and be encouraged to set measurable goals for giving and receiving love.

Build Community Through Serving and Being Served

Community is about serving and humbly allowing others to serve you. The single most stirring example of this is recorded in John 13, where Jesus takes the position of the lowest servant and washes the feet of his followers. He gives them a powerful example and then calls them to follow. Servanthood is at the very core of community. To sustain deep relationships over a long period of time, there must be humility and a willingness to serve each other.

At the close of each session will be a clear challenge to servanthood. As a group, and as individual followers of Christ, you will discover that community is built through serving others. You will also find that your own small group members will grow in their ability to extend service to your life.

Bible Study Basics

To get the most out of this study, you will need to prepare and participate. Here are some guidelines to help you.

Preparing for the Study

1. If possible, even if you are not the leader, look over each session before you meet, read the Bible passages, and answer the questions. The more you are prepared, the more you will gain from the study.
2. Begin your preparation with prayer. Ask God to help you understand the passage and apply it to your life.
3. A good modern translation, such as the New International Version, Today's New International Version, the New American Standard Bible, or the New Revised Standard Version, will give you the most help. Questions in this guide are based on the New International Version.
4. Read and reread the passages. You must know what the passage says before you can understand what it means and how it applies to you.
5. Write your answers in the spaces provided in the study guide. This will help you participate more fully in the discussion and will also help you personalize what you are learning.
6. Keep a Bible dictionary handy to look up unfamiliar words, names, or places.

Participating in the Study

1. Be willing to join in the discussion. The leader of the group will not be lecturing but will encourage people to discuss what they have learned in the passage. Plan to share what God has taught you during your preparation time.
2. Stick to the passages being studied. Base your answers on the verses being discussed rather than on outside authorities such as commentaries or your favorite author or speaker.

3. Try to be sensitive to the other members of the group. Listen attentively when they speak, and be affirming whenever you can. This will encourage more hesitant members of the group to participate.
4. Be careful not to dominate the discussion. By all means participate, but allow others to have equal time.
5. If you are a discussion leader or a participant who wants further insights, you will find additional comments in the Leader's Notes at the back of the book.

Ten Commandments: Laws That Liberate

Early one morning, I was driving on a busy interstate by the southern tip of Lake Michigan. The conditions were stormy and some severe weather was blowing in off the lake. As I headed westbound toward Chicago, the sun suddenly cleared the horizon in the eastern sky behind me. The burst of high-intensity brilliance caused the autumn leaves along the side of the road to explode into a thousand varying hues. Moments later, against the backdrop of a dark gray-black sky, a dazzling double rainbow appeared. It was breathtaking. The people in the cars around me began honking their horns, pointing, and pounding on their steering wheels in amazement. It was as if all the people seeing this vision of beauty had to verify with the other drivers that they were really seeing what they thought they were seeing. In those few moments on that busy interstate I was gripped by the greatness of God. There was an impromptu worship service I will never forget.

A few decades ago a hard-hearted attorney of national fame sat in his car in a driveway and faced a moment of reckoning. His sins and lawbreaking activities had been discovered and would be splashed all over newspapers, magazine covers, and TV screens in a matter of days. He realized that in spite of the extensiveness of his wrongs and criminal behavior, there was a God whose love was greater than his sin. In that moment of personal turmoil and guilt, Chuck Colson was gripped to the core of his being by the greatness of God's compassion for sinners like himself. There was an unplanned worship service in that driveway with only one person in attendance.

These two scenarios, and countless others like them, remind us that God loves to catch us off guard and ambush us with his glory, compassion, love, and beauty. In these treasured moments we can feel strangely finite, profoundly vulnerable, spiritually tender, and quietly reverent before God. In these treasured moments, we understand that God is dynamic and awe-inspiring. In fact, in these moments, God seems a lot like … God. When the veil is lifted and we get these glimpses of glory we see that God is powerful, transcendent, unpredictable, even a little bit dangerous. At the same time we gain a deeper understanding that this amazing God is personal, compassionate, gracious, close at hand. Whenever we have a close encounter with God, we come away with a full awareness that we are the creatures and he is the transcendent Creator.

Thousands of years ago Moses had a powerful encounter with God. The Maker of heaven and earth revealed his glory, presence, and truth. He gave Moses the Ten Commandments. Each of these commandments reveals something about God, gives us direction, and moves us to a place of awestruck wonder and worship.

The first four commandments are vertical in nature, focusing on how we relate to God. The first commandment calls us to honor God as God, making sure we only worship the true God and never substitute lesser gods for him. The second warns never to reduce God by representing him with an image. The third calls us to honor God's name and never use it carelessly. The fourth teaches that wise people will remember the Sabbath day. Every seven days we are to stop working and invest a full day recalibrating our life, mind, and values around what is most important. If we follow the teaching of these first four commandments, our vertical relationship with God will be well on its way to health and strength.

The other six commandments are about our horizontal relationships, intended to provide direction for how we relate to other people. The order of the commandments is not accidental. First we deal with the vertical, then the horizontal. If we get our relationship with God right, we will be able to draw on his strength and wisdom as we seek to build God-honoring relationships with people. When our vertical relationship is whole and growing, we'll want to reflect God's holiness and grace by not dishonoring our parents, committing murder or adultery, stealing, lying, or coveting. As we walk closely with God, we feel satisfied by his presence, power, and provision.

My prayer is that in these six sessions you will meet God as Moses did; that you will see his glory, drink in his wisdom, and taste his truth. As you do, may you find yourself ambushed by God's glory and swept into the river of his grace.

Honor God as God

EXODUS 20:1–7

What can you learn from simply overhearing a few sentences, short fragments of a conversation? None of us would intentionally eavesdrop on someone else (I hope), but we do pick up pieces of conversations unintentionally when we find ourselves in places where proximity makes it impossible to block out all the chatter around us.

Below is a simple test to see how observant you are in these situations. Each of the following eight statements gives insight into a person's profession or interests. Just a line or two can give us perspective on what someone does, enjoys … even their character. But some of these statements might go over our heads entirely … if we don't understand the words and their meaning.

1. "Spec buying has pretty much squeezed the shorts out of the action."
2. "Interfaces to such service modules as database handlers can be packaged using macros."
3. "Cantilever those joists."
4. "Fifty percent of the line is a facultative placement and the other 50 percent is on a treaty with an excess loss provision of one million."
5. "She'll require an equilibration before any final restoration."
6. "I ordered a CBC."
7. "The kerygmatic imperative is teleologically soteriological."
8. "The APGAR score was nine."

The first three of the Ten Commandments, in a handful of words, reveal much about the heart of God. If we understand their meaning, our life and faith can change forever; if we don't, we will miss out on a lot more than just a few words or helpful advice. Consider these three statements:

1. You shall have no other gods before me.
2. You shall not make for yourself an idol.
3. You shall not misuse the name of the Lord your God.

God wants us to hear these words with open ears, minds, and hearts. And, more than that, he wants us to be formed and transformed by them.

NOTE: *Just for fun, the occupations represented by the eight statements on page 15 are listed under question 1 in the Leader's Notes.*

Making the Connection

1. Every occupation and walk of life has its own lingo. What is an example of the unique vocabulary used in your profession or vocation?

How can using this kind of shorthand or inside vocabulary be helpful in a specific line of work?

Knowing and Being Known

Read Exodus 20:1 – 7

2. Each of these first three commandments is phrased as a "shall not." What specific things do you believe God is saying we should *not* do when he declares . . .

   - Have no other gods before me.
   - Do not make for yourself an idol.
   - Do not misuse the name of God.

3. To every "You shall not," there is an implied "You shall." What specific things do you believe God is saying we *should do* when he declares . . .

   - Have no other gods before me.
   - Do not make for yourself an idol.
   - Do not misuse the name of God.

The First Commandment . . . Honor God as God

The What. God is instructing every person on the face of this earth to honor him as God. We are to acknowledge his existence, affirm his sovereignty, obey his directives, and honor him by giving the ultimate affection of our heart to him and no one else. He is saying, "Don't worship the sun, the moon, or the stars. Don't worship Baal, Molech, Dagon, or any false god of the ancient people. Don't give praise to Allah, Buddha, or any

(cont.)

figurehead of the world religions. Don't give your unyielding devotion to Lenin, Marx, Mao, any president, monarch, or political figure. Don't idolize sports heroes, movie stars, billionaires, or any person no matter what their source of fame." Nothing and no one should demand our ultimate allegiance ... except God! We are not to worship material goods, pleasure, power, fame, money, fashion, people's applause, or ourselves. We are to worship God, the only true God.

The Why. Why is God so concerned about our worshiping only him? It sounds a bit exclusive, doesn't it? Other deities do not threaten God; he knows they are not real. We are not dealing with an insecure God who must protect his divine ego by placing restrictions on our worship. So, what is going on here? When we read the Bible, it becomes clear that the primary reason God instructs human beings to worship him alone is that he knows wherever else we focus our ultimate allegiance will only lead to terrible disappointment ... now and for eternity. Putting it another way, whatever other god you bow down to will never come through for you in your deepest times of need.

The How. The biggest way we honor God as God is to believe his assessment of our sinful condition. Own it, repent of it, and turn to Christ for forgiveness and salvation. Once we have done this, we can learn to honor him as God in many other ways. We can lift up passionate and exclusive worship, in his name alone. We can pray to him as the only One who hears and answers us. We can tell the world about the one true God who loves people and came to save us from all of our wrongs.

Read Exodus 20:1 – 7; Psalm 115; and Isaiah 46:1 – 10

4. How do the first three commandments relate to each other and give us a whole and healthy sense of how we are to honor God as God?

5. What contrasts do Psalm 115 and Isaiah 46:1–10 draw between idols (false gods) and the true God of heaven?

    Idols: *The True God:*

    What do the contrasts in these passages teach you about the wisdom of following God and the folly of bowing down to idols?

6. What are some practical ways we can make sure God comes first in our life and no one and nothing else takes his place?

The Second Commandment ... Don't Try to Reduce God

The What. In God's infinite wisdom, he knew that no image crafted by human hands could ever accurately represent the totality of who he is. Nothing we humans could ever carve, mold, chisel, paint, or sculpt could begin to capture even a fraction of our transcendent God. Any image attempting to represent God would be grossly inadequate and automatically reduce or shrink him.

The Why. Images of God are automatically reductionary. They only convey a slice of the whole, and that's why we should be careful with the

(cont.)

---

use of religious symbols, relics, icons, altars, and a host of other objects. We need to be careful that we don't present any physical thing as somehow representing God, because the moment we do, we invite people to worship an idol.

The How. We are wise to refrain from the use of religious symbols of any kind if they have potential to become the focus of our worship. Every church, every individual needs to grapple with what this means for them. We don't need equipment in order to connect with God. We can come as we are, wherever we are, devoid of all the images, relics, or objects that often accompany religious expression. We can come to God while standing on an assembly line, while driving a car, while working at home, on our way to class, or anywhere else we might go. We don't need beads, basins, crosses, or candelabras. God invites us: "Come to me as you are, where you are, with a repentant and contrite heart, and I will make myself real to you."

Read Exodus 20:4 – 6

7. What are some of the objects, pieces of furniture in a church building, or religious symbols that can become the focal point of our worship if we are not careful? Why is it dangerous to give "sacred status" to these objects?

8. Many people are bothered when God says, "I, the Lord your God, am a jealous God." The term "jealous" is not to be understood in the crude sense that people can be jealous of one another. God's holy jealousy is a sign of his commitment to protect his own name and character. What is the Lord communicating about himself when he declares that he is a jealous God?

9. God draws an amazing contrast in this second commandment. The consequences of sin might trickle down for a few generations, but his love cascades like a waterfall for a thousand generations. How have you seen the love of God pour from one generation to the next?

The Third Commandment ... Revere God's Name

The What. God says to everybody, "Never use my name as a form of cursing. Do not use it as an outlet for anger or as an expression of outrage." And to believers God says, "Don't even use my name carelessly in a prayer, a song, or any conversation — be careful with my name."

The Why. When we use a person's name we bring to mind the essence of who that person is. When someone says the name Martin Luther King Jr., we all automatically think of civil rights and the terrible sins of racism and discrimination; we recall King's character, life, and legacy. When someone says the name of Jesus or God, it should be an occasion to remember the love, grace, and truth that God brings into the world. God's name should lead us to praise and worship. To use the name of God as a curse or form of profanity is diametrically opposed to the character of the One whose name we are using.

The How. In the Lord's Prayer, Jesus taught his followers to pray, "Our Father in heaven, hallowed be your name" (Matthew 6:9). According to Malachi 1:10–14, we profane, or take in vain, the name of God whenever we do not represent him well to others in word, worship, or action. The best way to avoid misusing God's name is to remember who he is — his character, his mighty works on our behalf. When we do, we will lift up praises instead of curses.

Read Exodus 20:7

10. Why do you think so many people (even Christians) feel free to use God's name as profanity?

How do you think God feels about people using his name in this way?

11. What are ways we can lift up and honor the name of God, and treat the name of Jesus as holy and precious?

Celebrating and Being Celebrated

Take time as a small group to pray in the following ways:
- Thank God that he is the one true God. Praise him for revealing himself to you.
- Pray for wisdom to see where any form of idolatry is creeping into your heart and ask for strength to get rid of it.
- Praise God for his many names and the character they reveal. Think of a biblical name for God and lift it up, praising him for what you learn about him because he is: Prince of Peace, Father, the Good Shepherd, etc.

Loving and Being Loved

We are to do more than simply put God first. We should monitor very closely whatever seems to be vying consistently for second place in our life, because a second-place contender can quickly overtake God's rightful place if we are not watchful and diligent.

During the next week make a list of those things that contend for second place in your life, whether people, hobbies, work, or entertainments (anything that can monopolize your heart and time).

Things that can fight for second or first place in my life:

- _____
- _____
- _____

Identify ways you can press these things back when they fight for supremacy in your heart and life, so you will keep God first.

Serving and Being Served

One of the best ways we can serve the world, specifically those who do not have faith in God, is to model what it means to honor the name of the Lord. In the coming month, seek to do these two things:

1. Evaluate your speech to make sure you never misuse God's name in frustration, in casual unawareness, or in moments of surprise or anger. If you do, seek to purge these phrases from your vocabulary. Notice any time you use the name of Jesus or God in an unflattering way and commit to avoid these expressions.

2. Look for opportunities to bless the name of God and mention his character in positive ways. In particular, since the name of God is really about his character, lift up elements of God's attributes when it is natural to do so. For instance, when you see something beautiful, intricate, or

powerful in creation, express your appreciation for God as an amazing Creator. Or, when you have tasted God's grace or mercy in a tangible way, speak of it and point to God as the giver of these good gifts.

Remember the Sabbath

EXODUS 20:8–11

In the beginning, when God created paradise, there was a man, a woman, a beautiful garden, the complete absence of sin, and work. That's right, work was introduced to the human experience *before* sin shattered perfection—work shows up in Genesis 2:15, sin not until Genesis 3:6. In other words, labor is not a result of the fall and sin; it is a good gift from God.

During creation God designed this wonderful thing called human labor. He offered it to men and women as a gift that enables us to feel purposeful and useful here on earth. This gift challenges us to identify our unique abilities and develop our God-given potential. Work allows us to add value to our life and the lives of others. It even provides food on the table and resources on which to live.

But, as with other good gifts from God, human beings throughout the course of history have tended to find ways to turn this blessing into a curse. Many people have reduced the broad horizons of human reality into this one narrow dimension. These people order their lives around their work. They shape their relationships around their occupation. They wound their spouse and children because of their commitment to vocation. They ruin their bodies because they don't know how to hit the brake and stop working. Sadly, some even lose their souls because they squeeze God out of their consciousness, schedule, and heart due to their all-consuming commitment to their work.

Because God can see our propensity to become obsessed with work, he gave us the fourth commandment: to take a day off, a Sabbath, every seven days. Not only does God command us to cease laboring every Sabbath day, but he modeled this practice for us when he made the heavens and the earth. After six days of amazing creativity and productive work, God rested on the seventh day. He wasn't tired or weary. He did not need a day off. Instead, he was modeling behavior for his children, like all good parents do.

Making the Connection

1. What are some possible consequences if a person becomes obsessed with their work (no matter how important it might be) and won't take a regular Sabbath day?

Knowing and Being Known

Read Genesis 2:2 – 3; Exodus 20:8 – 11; and Hebrews 4:9 – 11

2. What are some of the guidelines God gives for keeping the Sabbath, and why do you think these are important?

If your family had Sabbath guidelines when you were growing up, what were they and how do they line up with what the Bible teaches about the Sabbath?

3. Parents serve as models for their children. Dad will tie his own shoe over and over again to help his son get the idea. Mom will take a big bite of baby food trying to convince her finicky six-month-old to eat the "delicious pureed green beans." Why should God's model of Sabbath rest inspire his children to take the call to Sabbath seriously?

With God's example and a clear call to establish a pattern of Sabbath rest in our life, why do so many of us avoid this practice?

More to Life Than Labor

God commands the cessation of labor every seventh day as a reminder that there is more to life than human labor. Recognition, honor, power, and money will keep a good number of people motivated well past closing time. Before we know it, everything else and everyone else in life pales in comparison to the addictive aspects of our work. God calls us to Sabbath in an effort to keep us from making the dreadful reductionary error of believing our whole existence is about work.

William Wilberforce, a nineteenth-century member of English Parliament, is widely remembered for his legislative labors that eventually outlawed slavery in the British Empire. By his own admission, Wilberforce had a terrible time controlling his own ambitions. He worked hard to rise to positions of power and influence so that he could make decisions he felt would be good for the country and the world. In one particular era of his life, when his runaway ambition was threatening his health and even his soul, he wrote this entry in his journal: "Blessing be to God for the day of rest and religious occupation wherein earthly things assume their true size, and ambition is stunted." In essence, Wilberforce was saying that the Sabbath day was a kind of built-in check-and-balance system that enabled him to keep his career in proper perspective.

4. The teaching of Scripture paints a picture of people who work hard but who also know how to rest and unplug. In other words, work and rest do not have to be enemies. How have you learned to strike a healthy equilibrium between your work and experiencing the blessing of rest that God offers to his children?

5. William Wilberforce wrote, "Blessing be to God for the day of rest and religious occupation wherein earthly things assume their true size, and ambition is stunted." When you take a day off, a season of vacation, or a regular Sabbath day, how does this time of quiet and the margin it affords help things "assume their true size"?

How can Sabbath put the brakes on human ambition and bring perspective when we are living with pathological busyness?

Connect with God and People

The fourth commandment says that the Sabbath should be " ... to the Lord your God." Sabbath is not just about ceasing from labor; the margin this discipline provides makes space to spend quality time connecting intimately with our Creator. Indeed, every day should include a mini Sabbath when we yield to the Lord in prayer and pour out our hearts to him. This time gives us strength for the challenges of daily life, connecting us to the Source of wisdom, motivation, virtue, and grace. Scripture also states clearly that God's people should come together on a weekly basis for the purpose of remembering God as a community. This was the custom throughout the Old Testament, the New Testament, and the history of the church. The Sabbath is a gift because it affords time for us to connect with God personally and in community with other Christ followers.

Read Hebrews 10:24 – 25 and Acts 2:42 – 47

6. What ways have you found to connect with God in your personal relationship with him?

How do you seek to incorporate these in your Sabbath day?

7. Meeting God in community is clearly part of his design for how we connect with him as we slow down and observe Sabbath. What happens when we are in community that simply can't happen when we are alone?

What do you think God might say to a person who declares, "I meet with God best when I am all alone in the quietness of my home, or out in creation. I really don't like gathering with other Christians"?

Time to Recalibrate Your Life

Smaller private airplanes have two compasses on the instrument panel. One is a conventional floating-ball compass, the kind you might see on a car dashboard. The other is called a gyrocompass, which is a lot easier to read and to use for navigation. This kind of compass must be recalibrated with the main compass every fifteen to twenty minutes in order for it to be of value. If not, a pilot could end up drifting far off-course. The same is true of every aspect of our lives, including the spiritual dynamics. Our lives require almost constant recalibration. Certainly, a weekly Sabbath is a great time to let God take us through a process of recalibration.

Read Matthew 11:28 – 30 and Psalm 127:1 – 2

8. Which aspect of your life tends to drift out of calibration the quickest, and how might a weekly Sabbath provide time to recalibrate?

    • Commitment to your family
    • Commitment to take care of your physical health
    • Time with friends
    • Time sitting at the feet of Jesus
    • Another area of your life _____

9. Sabbath is not about a rigid set of rules and regulations or about one set day that all people must observe (see Leader's Note for question 1). It is about establishing a rhythm of life where one in every seven days we have time/margin to recalibrate our life and soul. What tends to be the best day of the week for you to take a Sabbath and why?

The Gift of Refreshment

The Sabbath, this wonderful gift from God, gives us space to connect with our Creator, be in community with other believers, and recalibrate our lives. While this is all true, there is another great benefit of observing the Sabbath. This is a day when we can experience peace, joy, and refreshment, when we can recharge our batteries and bring freshness to our soul.

For some people this happens as they take a long walk. For others, taking a bike ride does the job. People get refreshed by playing in the snow, being out on a boat, taking an afternoon nap, gardening, engaging in a family activity, sharing a meal with close friends, enjoying a recreational pursuit, reading a book; the list could go on for pages. Whatever it is that reenergizes you, that rejuvenates your body and mind, God says, "That's what I want you to do. Make that a portion of your Sabbath experience." God's desire is that you would be thoroughly refreshed and rejuvenated by the end of your weekly Sabbath observance.

10. What is one thing that refreshes you, recharges your batteries, and rejuvenates your soul?

How could you incorporate this in your Sabbath experience more consistently?

11. What is something that tries to slip into your Sabbath day but tends to deplete your energy reserves and does not rejuvenate your soul?

What can you do to guard your Sabbath day from being invaded by this kind of activity or engagement?

Celebrating and Being Celebrated

Take time as a group to pray in these three directions:
- As William Wilberforce did, thank God for a day that he has given to you to put life back in perspective.
- If you have been letting the pressures of life and demands of work push Sabbath to the side, confess this to God and ask for strength to reestablish a weekly Sabbath day.
- Pray for your group members to have glorious and sweet days of Sabbath that really do connect them to God and to other people, and that recalibrate their lives.

Loving and Being Loved

Your heavenly Father took a Sabbath day for the sake of modeling this life rhythm for his children ... for you. God chose to make Sabbath observance one of his "top ten" commandments for all of his people. He knows you better than you know yourself. He made you for more than work! Show love to your heavenly Father by following his call to experience Sabbath rest one day out of every seven.

As an act of love toward God, sit down with a calendar for the coming four weeks and block out one full day each week as a Sabbath. If you have work scheduled for these days, cancel it if you can. If you have meetings, reschedule them. If you have housework, yard work, homework, freelance work, or any other work blocked out for this day, push it to another time. Really open the day up for the things discussed in this session. Plan to do something that refreshes you. Make space to connect with God. Plan to be with God's people in some capacity. Try being a man or woman of Sabbath for one full month and see what God does in your heart and life through this commitment. As you do this, know that your Father in heaven will take joy in your efforts to do what he did and be more like him!

Serving and Being Served

If you have a spouse, family member, or friend who is overextended and needs to get back to a rhythm of Sabbath, offer to help them. Ask what you might do to alleviate their workload and free them to take a Sabbath. As they set a day aside to enjoy God, people, and refreshment, commit to pray for them to be so blessed on this day that they commit to make it a weekly spiritual discipline.

Honor Your Parents

EXODUS 20:12; EPHESIANS 6:1–3

It's no accident that the fifth commandment made the "top ten." God knows better than we do that family matters are of great importance. The family is the basic social unit of a healthy society, the birthplace of life-giving values such as honor, respect, and self-esteem. Loving parents who raise godly children build a launch pad for every area of life.

Think about the example of Jesus. As he drew near the end of his life—hanging on a cross, the depravity of the entire human race about to fall on him like an avalanche—he choked out only seven short phrases, and one of them was concern for his mother. His heart ached for the woman who had raised him, loved him, and followed her Son up the hill called Golgotha. He knew she needed someone to look out for her. In John's gospel we read:

> Near the cross of Jesus stood his mother, his mother's sister, Mary the wife of Clopas, and Mary Magdalene. When Jesus saw his mother there, and the disciple whom he loved standing nearby, he said to his mother, "Dear woman, here is your son," and to the disciple, "Here is your mother." From that time on, this disciple took her into his home. (19:25–27)

Jesus was saying, "John, take care of my mom. Look after her. She will need you after I am gone." He was also saying, "Mom, John will be there for you. He will care for you like a son would after I am gone." What a staggeringly beautiful picture! What an example of honoring a parent ... even in a time of excruciating pain.

35

Making the Connection

1. What is one thing about your parents that makes it easy to honor them?

What are some challenges people might face in their growing-up years that can make it hard to honor their parents?

Knowing and Being Known

Read Exodus 20:12 and Ephesians 6:1 – 3

2. What is the promise that comes when children obey their parents in the Lord, and how would you describe the heartbeat of this promise?

What is the distinction between simply obeying your parents and obeying them "in the Lord"?

3. How have you seen this promise fulfilled in the lives of people who obey this commandment and seek to live in ways that honor their parents?

Honoring Parents Through the Seasons of Life

Honoring Parents During Childhood. The fifth commandment is carried out differently in the various stages of life. During the early childhood years, the way we honor our parents is to simply obey them, to do what they say. God knows that children have a sin nature and that this rebel streak will lead to poor choices and pain. Parents have a calling from God to carefully and consistently protect their children from the destructive force of sin. God counsels parents to draw boundaries, discipline with love, nurture in the faith, and give godly leadership. As parents do this, children are called to honor their parents by obeying them.

Honoring Parents During the Adolescent Years. This stage of life, which includes the high school years and even young adulthood, takes a different slant. Honoring parents moves from simple obedience to respect and cooperation. Young adults no longer need constant supervision and a long list of do's and don'ts; they begin to make some of their own decisions as they establish their identity apart from Dad and Mom. In this season of life, children will invariably disagree with their parents; that's a part of the separation process. But adolescents can still be respectful. God commands adolescents to honor their parents by negotiating this wrenching era of their life with a sense of grace and honor, respect and cooperation. God says to adolescents, "Even during this troublesome, turbulent time, obey the fifth commandment."

Honoring Parents During the Adult Years. The fifth commandment does not become null and void when we leave home for households, families, and careers of our own. This commandment is binding as long as our parents are alive. A great word to describe what it means to honor parents when we are adults is "treasure." We are to treasure our father and

(cont.)

mother in their later years. As we begin to build our lives and raise children, we come to terms with all the service and sacrifice that went into our own development. We have these moments of awakening about how much love, time, energy, and effort our parents invested in us. In this season we can say thank you and treasure the ones who poured themselves into us in our younger years.

4. If you were to sit down with a child and encourage them in how to honor their parents, what advice would you give them?

What are some of the benefits of children honoring and obeying their parents?

5. What might you say to a teenager who declares *one* of following?

   • "I can't get along with my parents because they are so out of touch with my world and what really matters to me."

- "My parents give me too many boundaries. All they do is tell me, 'Stop doing that!' I think they are out to ruin my life and make sure I never have any fun."

- "If I have to listen to my parents tell me one more story about how they experienced the same things I am going through I am going to scream! My parents have no clue what I am facing today."

- "My parents claim that they tell me no for my own good. All I know is that it does not feel like they are really concerned about me."

What are some of the benefits of adolescents respecting and cooperating with their parents?

6. Name some practical ways adult children can honor their parents and show them that they are treasured, valued, and appreciated.

7. Every earthly father and mother makes mistakes. No parent is perfect. What are ways we can honor parents even when they have hurt us in deep ways?

Steps to Restoration

Many people are living pain-filled lives, driven by bitterness and constant struggle because they were not cherished, protected, and loved by their parents. Due to neglect or abuse, deep hurt seems to impact every aspect of life. This can lead to addictive lifestyles, abusive behaviors, emotional distance from others, and more. There are no simple answers to the brokenness some people face in their relationships with parents, but the following steps might help us move forward:

1. Admit your pain, own it, and let yourself grieve. Don't bury it and act like it never happened. Bring it to God, and admit that you have been deeply hurt.

2. You may want to talk with your parents about how you feel and what you experienced in your home that brought pain in your life. If it is possible, sit face-to-face and let them know how you have been hurt and the impact it has had on your life.
3. Ask God to help you forgive. Forgiving does not mean what they did was right, but it does mean that you will no longer let their past behavior poison your present and future.
4. Connect with a godly and mature member of your church who can come alongside you to offer prayer, encouragement, and support. Don't carry this burden alone. If you have a confidential and trustworthy small group, you might want to invite their care and support as well.
5. Contact a professional Christian counselor to help you process your past experiences and move toward wholeness.

Read Galatians 6:2; Colossians 3:13; and I Peter 2:23 – 25

8. If you have faced pain in your relationship with your parents, what steps have you taken toward healing, and how has God grown your ability to love and honor this parent?

9. Some people have been hurt so deeply that they are sure there is no way they could ever forgive the parent who wronged them. What are some of the potential negative consequences if we refuse to forgive and seek a restored relationship with a parent who has hurt us?

How does Jesus' example toward those who hurt and abused him inform this discussion? (Remember, because of our sins, we are numbered among those who put Jesus on the cross.)

Never Forget, You Have a Father in Heaven!

Whatever kind of earthly parenting we had, we can all take comfort in knowing that we have an honorable heavenly Father who loves us perfectly. He knows our deepest needs and tender spots; he cares about our wounds and scars, our struggles and hidden sins. Despite our flaws and failures, he gladly calls us his sons and daughters. He wants us to know that there is no other love that compares to his fatherly compassion for us. He is ready to make his presence known, comfort and console, encourage and affirm, provide and protect, guide and guard, instruct and inspire. His love is so great that he opened the way to eternity, through the death and resurrection of Jesus, so that we could be with him forever.

Read Matthew 6:9; Galatians 4:6 – 7; and Colossians 1:10 – 14

10. How has the love of your heavenly Father helped strengthen and carry you through the times when others (including earthly parents) have not been there for you?

11. How does building a strong and healthy relationship with your heavenly Father strengthen you as you seek to follow the fifth commandment?

Celebrating and Being Celebrated

Take time as a group to offer prayers of thanks and appreciation for:

- Mothers who have been loving, kind, and a strong presence in your life.
- Fathers who have loved, cared, provided, and walked with you.
- Your heavenly Father, who was been your Abba and protector through life.

Loving and Being Loved

If one (or both) of your parents is still living, take time in the coming week to let them know how much you appreciate the role they have played, and still play, in your life. Write a note, make a phone call, send a small but thoughtful gift, or take them out for lunch. Be sure to articulate specific ways God has blessed your life through them. Remember, no parent is perfect. Expressing appreciation for one way they have parented you does not mean you are saying they were perfect in every way. It is simply an act of honoring what you can at this point in your relationship.

Serving and Being Served

In many of our lives, God provides spiritual parents who come alongside us in our times of need. These Christian "mothers and fathers" mean so much to us. For those who lived with deep pain in their home of origin, or who grew up with nonbelieving parents, spiritual parents give us a picture of God's fatherly love. If you have been blessed with such a person in your life, make a point of doing something special for them. Let them know how God has shaped your heart and strengthened your soul through them.

Protect and Honor Life

EXODUS 20:13–14; MATTHEW 5:21–30

I am fully convinced that if Jesus Christ were with us today and taught on the sixth and seventh commandments, at some point in his sermon he would say, "Friends, look around you because there are murderers and adulterers everywhere." Most of us would shift rather uneasily in our seats, take quick glances around, and wonder who Jesus was talking about. If we listened closely to the words of the Savior we would eventually have a moment of clarity ... we would realize that Jesus was talking about us!

When Jesus preached he would often make a very strong point that forced people to look beyond the obvious and discover a deeper understanding of how sin was at work in their hearts and lives. One topic addressed all through the Bible is the value of human life. God calls each of his people to do all we can to protect and honor life. This is why God made these two brief and simple statements:

The sixth commandment ... *You shall not murder.*
The seventh commandment ... *You shall not commit adultery.*

Given to Moses on Mount Sinai, these are crystal-clear calls to honor and protect life.

But by the days of Jesus, many people looked at these commandments as applying only to those who had murdered another person with their own hands or who had violated the marriage covenant through the act of sexual adultery. Jesus wanted them, *and us*, to know that the call to honor life goes much deeper than simply refraining from the acts of murder or adultery. Hatred in our hearts and harsh words toward others are another form of murder just as lusting in our hearts and allowing ungodly sexual scenarios to run though our minds are another form of adultery.

In the English language, the sixth and seventh commandments are expressed in only nine words. But when we break these commandments they can bring damage and pain to people that can't be expressed in a million words.

Making the Connection

1. Imagine a world where murder and adultery were deemed acceptable and normal behavior. What implications would this have on a society?

Knowing and Being Known

Read Exodus 20:13 – 14 and Matthew 5:21 – 30

2. How does Jesus' teaching on the sixth commandment, "You shall not murder," deepen your understanding of what it means in your daily life?

What are examples of how some people break the sixth commandment and don't even realize they are doing it?

3. How does Jesus' teaching on the seventh commandment, "You shall not commit adultery," deepen your understanding of what it means in your daily life?

What are examples of how some people break the seventh commandment and don't even realize they are doing it?

Don't Take Life

Have you ever imagined what the first homicide was like? You don't have to travel very far into human history—Genesis 4—before it happened. One man took the life of another. Cain killed his brother Abel in a jealous rage. Adam and Eve beheld death for the first time. Heaven and earth must have looked on in numb shock at the sight of it all and wondered, "Who does Cain think he is? No one has the right to pirate God's prerogative to number a man's days. No one."

By logical extension this commandment covers many expressions of the human propensity to take life. Many respected scholars and theologians are confident that in this sixth commandment God is saying:

- Don't number your own days and take your own life (suicide).
- Don't end the life of the unborn when it is still in the womb (abortion).
- Don't take the life of the newly born (infanticide).
- Don't shorten the life of the elderly, even when life gets hard (euthanasia).
- Don't take the life of another person in anger, jealousy, or revenge (murder).

(cont.)

God is the Lord of life, and he is clear that it is not our role or prerogative to step in and take his place. As we seek to follow the sixth commandment we see the need to honor and protect life. In a very practical way, this means that we never take the life of another person into our own hands.

Read Exodus 20:13 and Matthew 5:21 – 26

4. What are some of the signs that people are growing more relaxed about breaking the sixth commandment? (Think about the five bullet points in the text box above.)

5. How can Christians take actions and actively work for causes that will protect human life?

Don't Kill in Your Heart or with Your Words

Jesus sobered a self-righteous crowd one day when he declared that there is a frightening similarity between physical and verbal violence. In other words, Jesus wanted us to know that murdering with our hands and killing someone with our words are both sin.

There is a close connection between a crimson, dripping knife and juicy gossip. There is a link between bullets and bad-mouthing. All of these behaviors emanate from a hate-filled heart. Jesus wants us to know that we can kill a person with our hands or with our words, and he forbids both kinds of violence.

Read Proverbs 12:18; Proverbs 18:21; and James 3:3 – 12

6. How have you seen people be cut, wounded, and devastated by the words of others?

    How does God feel about holding hatred in one's heart and lashing out with hurtful words?

7. What can we do to guard our mouths and thus make sure we do not break the sixth commandment by attacking people with words?

    How can we use our words to bring healing, blessing, and life to others?

Honor Life as You Restrain Sexual Desires

Our sexual desires are more complex and powerful than most of us realize. Sexual expression between a man and a woman within the covenant of marriage is honoring and pleasing to God. But breaking God's boundaries for our sexuality is an assault on his plan for human life. When a person gets emotionally entangled and then sexually involved with someone who is not their spouse, they are breaking the seventh commandment.

An "innocent little flirtation" can lead to a tragic moral fall; it happens all the time. This is one reason Jesus stressed that lust in our hearts is tantamount to adultery itself. Jesus was emphasizing the fact that once a person begins to fantasize about having an inappropriate sexual experience with another person, that man or woman is already on the road to pain and ruin. It's only a matter of time.

Read Exodus 20:14 and Matthew 5:27 – 30

8. How are the boundaries concerning sexuality being blurred and even removed in modern society?

How does this impact the way people understand the seventh commandment?

9. What do you think Jesus might say to a person who declares: "I am married and committed to my spouse, but there is nothing wrong with looking at other people. I can look all I want as long as I don't touch! What goes on in my mind and heart won't impact what I do"?

Swimming Upstream

It's becoming increasingly difficult to swim upstream in a society that's rushing downstream toward unrestricted sexual expression. Obeying the seventh commandment in today's culture will often be a lonely experience. Record numbers of people are violating the seventh commandment in action and in their hearts. Pornography and permissiveness are considered acceptable. Marriage relationships are becoming increasingly difficult. As communication in marriage breaks down, discouragement grows, and pressures mount, a third party looks more and more inviting. The enemy of our soul whispers in our ear, "It would be so refreshing, so exciting, so uncomplicated. What would it hurt? You deserve to be happy and have a little fun." What Satan never mentions is that this sexual sin will destroy the people we love the most.

Because of the wide-scale fragmentation of families and society over the last fifty years, healthy marriages are going to be more difficult. They will require higher levels of commitment. Building healthy and life-giving homes will demand swimming upstream.

10. What steps can we take to build strong marriages and protect ourselves from the temptations of sexual compromise?

11. What can Christian friends (and small group members) do to cheer each other on in the following areas?

- Helping married couples build stronger relationships and establish healthy boundaries with their sexual expression
- Encouraging single people to honor God with their sexuality and remain pure in their relational life
- Cheering on teens and young adults who are navigating the world of dating and finding a godly husband or wife
- Blessing those who feel called to a single life and cheering them on as they honor God in this calling

Celebrating and Being Celebrated

God is all about life. Even from the beginning, death was not his plan. One day, when Jesus returns and all things are made right, death will be gone and eternal life will be fully realized. As a group celebrate God's gift of life and his commitment to protect and honor it. Use some of the following prompts to spark your prayers:

- Thank you for giving life, for breathing breath into us, for starting it all.

- I praise you for the new life we have in Jesus and the hope that comes in his name.
- God, you have invited us into your work of protecting life. Thank you for trusting us to honor life and not destroy it.

Loving and Being Loved

If you are married, reflect on ways you can love your spouse with growing passion. Identify any emotional, relational, or even physical entanglements with someone other than your spouse. Repent of these things, turn from them, seek accountability, and return your heart fully to your spouse. Make time to date your spouse, speak words of grace and encouragement, nurture your physical and romantic relationship—whatever it takes to build a strong marriage. If things are broken, get help and fix them. Building a Christ-honoring marriage is worth the effort.

Serving and Being Served

As followers of Jesus we are called to do more than just express what we are against. If we are against killing, then we should stand for life. Consider serving occasionally in a ministry or community organization that honors and protects life. It could be an adoption organization, a group that helps girls and women find options other than abortion for unwanted pregnancies, a senior center designed to improve the quality of life for senior citizens, etc. As you stand for life, support those who are taking action to protect and honor life.

The Essential Place of Honesty

EXODUS 20:15–16

If you're looking to stimulate conversation in a social setting sometime, ask this question: "What are the most important qualities you look for when seeking to establish a new friendship?" Most people would place honesty somewhere near the top of their list.

On the flipside, pose this question to people who've been deeply hurt in a relationship: "What caused the deepest disappointment and the gradual demise of your relationship?" Within their answer you will usually hear words and phrases like: dishonesty, being lied to, feeling deceived.

It is almost impossible to overstate the amount of damage that occurs when deceit and betrayal are uncovered in a relationship. Most friendships, marriages, and business partnerships can withstand the periodic bumps and bruises brought about by misunderstandings and miscommunications. But when there is evidence of outright deception and bold-faced lying, chances are the relationship is headed for hard days. If the wound isn't fatal, the relationship will probably be in the intensive care ward a long, long time.

This is why God devotes two of the Ten Commandments to the topic of honesty. He calls us to be honest in our actions: "You shall not steal." He also commands us to be honest in our words: "You shall not give false testimony." If we can follow this wise counsel, it will do wonders for the health of all our relationships. If we ignore these commands, we will find our relationships shipwrecked on the rocky shores of dishonesty.

Making the Connection

1. Tell about a time when someone close to you was dishonest and hurt you with their words or actions.

How did this impact the health and future of your relationship?

Knowing and Being Known

Read Exodus 20:15 – 16

2. How does stealing damage a relationship and undermine honesty?

3. How can lying impact *one* of the following relationships?

   • When a child is caught lying to a parent

- When a spouse discovers that their husband/wife has been deceiving them

- When a friend realizes that they have not really known the truth about someone they thought was close and transparent with them

- When an employer discovers that an employee has been dishonest

Blatant Stealing

Some people steal through seizure or old-fashioned thievery. Probably the most graphic of all of Jesus' stories is the parable of the Good Samaritan (Luke 10:30–36). Thieves pounce on a man minding his own business; they beat him, take his goods, and leave him for dead. The Bible is clear that this kind of blatant thievery is a gross violation of the eighth commandment. Hopefully, most of us would identify such behavior as wrong and avoid it.

But other examples of stealing can often slip under our radar even though they dishonor God just as much. Some of us have taken company supplies and rationalized it as part of our pay. We use the company phone lines for personal calls and let the business cover the costs. We use a company gas card or expense account for something that is clearly not work related. We might borrow a neighbor's ladder, hedge clippers, saucepan, or punch bowl, and always forget to give it back. Or we borrow a friend's book, DVD, CD, sports equipment, or piece of jewelry, and over time it just becomes ours. We may not want to admit it, but these are all forms of stealing. These things break trust, reveal dishonesty, and damage relationships.

4. What are examples of stealing that have become so commonplace that many people no longer see these behaviors as wrong and offensive to God?

5. What are some actions and behaviors that will help Christians be honest, trustworthy, and above reproach when they're tempted to steal?

Subtle Stealing Through Deception

Another unbiblical means of acquiring things is through deception. This is not as blatant, but it is just as wrong. Proverbs 20:23 says, "The LORD detests differing weights, and dishonest scales do not please him." Over three millennia ago, business people doctored their scales to cheat consumers. This same thing goes on today ... people subtly cut corners and charge too much or do not give what has been promised. This is a form of breaking the eighth commandment.

False advertising, emotional hype, exaggerated promises, untrue claims, and countless other dishonest practices lead to stealing and distrust between people. It's a violation of God's law when: a salesman tells a customer to buy an additional insurance policy that is really unnecessary, a doctor recommends a pointless procedure, or a heating specialist deceitfully says, "I'd hate to head into winter with that kind of furnace in my basement, but then it's your life. How many kids do you have?" Deception is often just a sophisticated way of stealing people's money and attaining their property. God forbids it.

6. Some forms of stealing don't actually involve taking an item or object from someone, but a stealthy and subtle practice of deceit that manipulates us into buying what we don't need, paying more than something is worth, or making a purchase based on dishonest information. What practices and behaviors of subtle deception have you encountered?

7. What can we do to make sure we are not employing practices that are deceitful and break the trust of others?

Lies, Lies, and More Lies

At the beginning of time, Satan lied to Eve, telling her she would not die if she ate from the fruit of the tree in the middle of the garden. If you ever wonder how bad the consequences of lying can be, remember that we are still paying the consequences of that first lie!

People lie for all kinds of reasons. Sometimes we lie to impress people. We drop names and call people we barely know "close friends"; or we inflate numbers and statistics. Sometimes we lie to please people. We agree with strong-personality types in their presence and then kick ourselves privately for assenting to something we don't really believe. Sometimes we lie to get revenge. Someone hurts us and so we trump up a story or a rumor to get back at them. We lie to make a profit, to escape punishment; we even lie for convenience. All kinds of things can trigger a lie.

Read Ephesians 4:25

8. What are some examples of ways we can be tempted to lie for *one* of the following reasons?
   - To impress someone
   - To please people
   - To get back at someone
   - To escape punishment
   - For convenience

9. Lies have a way of snowballing and taking on a life of their own. Before we know it, we are buried under an avalanche of deception. How have you seen one lie end up growing into something much bigger than the original deception?

Stop the Lies

God wants his children to declare war on lying. The *first* step in doing this is to be ruthless with ourselves about our propensity to lie. We have to admit that we are all prone to dishonesty. *Second*, we need to commit to be truth-tellers. Integrity should mark our lives and guide our words. *Third*, we can invite consistent accountability. If we have been drawn into deceptive words in the past, we can let a close brother or sister know how we struggle and invite their prayers and accountability. *Finally*, when we do lie and speak with deception, we can confess it to God and to the person we lied to. We can clean up the mess by being a truth-teller.

10. How can each of these four guidelines help us cut off the temptation to lie?

- Admitting to ourselves and to God that we are prone to lie

- Committing to be a consistent truth-teller

- Inviting accountability in the things we say

- Confessing when we have lied

Celebrating and Being Celebrated

Take time as a group to share short testimonies with each other. In particular, tell stories of a person in your life who has lived as a model of honesty in their words as well as their lifestyle. Talk about how their life of integrity impacted you and shaped your view of how to treat people.

Loving and Being Loved

Sometime in the coming week, walk through your house, office, dorm room, even your garage and look for things that are not yours: Check your CDs and DVDs, your bookshelves and the clothes hanging in your closet. Whatever is not yours, return it. If it can't be returned, consider making restitution for it. Or if you can't find something you know you borrowed, get a replacement and give it to the person.

Instead of just giving the object back and saying, "I'm sorry," let this be a chance to tell someone about the difference your faith is making in your life. Let them know you are a follower of Jesus Christ and that your small group is studying the Ten Commandments. Tell them about what you are learning and how you are seeking to be honest as you respect other people's property. God might just use this to spark a spiritual conversation.

Serving and Being Served

One of the best ways to serve the people in your life is to live with honesty in your words and actions. Take time in the coming week to reflect on your life over the past month. (This is actually a variation of an age-old spiritual discipline known as a Review of the Day.) Think through conversations and interactions. Where you have been dishonest, confess this to God. Ask yourself questions such as:

- Was there the shadow of deception in my conversations?
- Did I mislead somebody?
- Was I trying to be diplomatic but did it border on being deceptive?
- Was I stretching the truth by only giving part of the story?

As you complete this moral inventory of what comes out of your mouth, do all you can to root the lies from your life.

Restrain Material Desires

EXODUS 20:17; COLOSSIANS 3:1–3

God created us to be creatures of desire. Stoics and Buddhists may attempt to extinguish the flames of desire from human personality, but our God chooses not to do that. Rather, he chooses to redirect the focus of human desire from that which is trivial and temporal to that which is weighty and eternal. God wants to use our passions and desires to accomplish his good purposes. But when our desires run wild, trouble is always near. That is why one fruit of the Holy Spirit is self-control—we need help as we seek to resist the human tendency to want what others have.

Every honest Christian will readily acknowledge how necessary the redirection and help of the Holy Spirit is. We have a fallen nature and we live in a broken world. Therefore, from time to time, we find ourselves consumed with the desire to possess something that has aroused our fancy. Sometimes the strength of that passion is so intense that it frightens us.

As if to pour gasoline on the flames of our sinful desires, professional marketing people are paid a lot of money to design billboards, commercials, and advertisements to amplify our desires. We watch a never-ending parade of new toys and "essential upgrades" marching in front of us. Combine our human tendency to always want more with the slick promotions of advertisers and a culture in love with material things, and it is no wonder that God warned us to be careful that we don't covet what is not ours.

Making the Connection

1. Give some examples of how coveting has become part of the fabric of our culture.

   How have you seen advertisers tap into the human tendency to covet, and how are their marketing strategies working?

Knowing and Being Known

Read Exodus 20:17; Matthew 6:24; I Timothy 6:6 – 10; and Hebrews 13:5

2. What contrast do you see between the love of God and the love of material things in these passages and elsewhere in the Bible?

3. Why do you think God gives such strong warnings against coveting or desiring more and more material things?

What are some ways people try to soften these warnings?

Why Restrain Material Desires?

If we are honest with ourselves, most of us would have to admit that we have a fascination with material things that has the potential of becoming a fixation. If we do not keep our desires in check and constantly monitor our tendency to covet, these material things can become larger than life. The tenth commandment's warning ("Never let goods turn into gods") is quite similar to the first's ("You shall have no other gods before me"). Bottom line, we should never allow our desire for acquisition to eclipse our ongoing desire to love and follow God. When we do, that grip on us is hard to loosen.

We are free to admire things for their beauty, value, or performance; there is no biblical prohibition against that. But covetousness digs its razor-sharp talons into our soul when harmless appreciation digresses into a frenzied need to possess. When this shift occurs, something has gone wrong in our heart. God says, "You've crossed the line. Your goods are becoming gods. This is the dangerous domain of coveting, and it is a form of idolatry."

Read Exodus 20:17 and Colossians 3:1 – 3

4. How have you seen goods become gods in your life or in the life of someone you know, and what were the consequences?

5. Using *one* of the scenarios below (or create your own), identify what it looks like when we cross the line from admi-
   ration/appreciation to covetousness. How does each one
   impact our neighbor and us?

   - *Scenario 1:* You have always liked classic cars and your
     neighbor just inherited two vintage cars from a family
     member.
   - *Scenario 2:* Your neighbor has a four-bedroom home
     and one child. You have three kids and a two-bedroom
     home. Now that same neighbor is talking about putting
     on an addition so they have some room to "spread out."

Fanning the Coveting Flame

No society in the history of civilization has faced the degree of temptation that this generation does when it comes to turning goods into gods.
We are bombarded with a full-fledged, frontal assault on our hearts every
day of our lives. From billboards to TV commercials to Internet pop-up
ads to radio plugs, it never seems to end.

You might say that most advertisers attempt to create covetousness
within us. It is their unabashed goal to arouse our passions, excite our
senses, and create a desire for their product that moves us to acquire
it, no matter the cost. Simply put, their goal is to fan the flames of our
desires enough to overpower our ability to say no to their pitch.

Read Romans 12:2

6. Tell about a time (as a child, teen, or adult) that a product promotion caught your imagination and really pulled you in.

What did you do to acquire this thing that seemed so important, and how did you feel when you finally got it?

7. How can we live with a healthy skepticism and wise filters when it comes to the advertisements and promotions that are designed to create covetousness?

Hitting Close to Home

Coveting, in a general sense, is a personal activity that leads us to want what is not ours. It is idolatry in the imagination of an individual. The tenth commandment narrows the focus and reveals something even closer to home. It speaks of a sinister form of coveting: wanting what belongs to your neighbor. There is no sin in admiring and appreciating that which is your neighbor's. But you cross the line when you begin to scheme up plans to **obtain** that which is your neighbor's.

This kind of coveting reveals a total disregard for the feelings of others. It reflects a lack of love. When you covet a neighbor's spouse, possessions, or anything they have, you have forgotten the call of Jesus to "love your neighbor as yourself" (Matthew 22:39). As this sinful desire grows unchecked in your soul, you're willing to hurt and bruise your neighbor just to get what you want. Untold pain and sorrow have been born of this human propensity toward coveting.

8. What do you think goes through the heart of God when his children walk around thinking things like:

  • If I had a house like Bill and Marsha's place, I could really be happy.
  • If I could just get the new computer all my friends have, I would never need another upgrade.
  • My neighbor does not deserve such a beautiful wife, great job, and nice car ... I wish I had his life.in

Contentment, the Antidote to Coveting

"Contentment" is considered a strange word in our coveting culture. When some people think of contentment they imagine someone who is slothful or lacks ambition, who doesn't have challenging goals or high aspirations. This is simply not true. The Bible defines contentment as having an inner sense of plenty no matter the outward circumstances.

Content people can have a lot or a little and still be at peace. The bottom line is that contentment is not based on what we have, but who has us! When Jesus has our heart and the Holy Spirit leads our lives, we are content. We know that everything that matters most is already signed, sealed, and delivered through the finished work of Jesus on the cross.

Read Philippians 4:12 – 13 and 1 Timothy 6:6 – 10

9. What are the distinctions between laziness (lack of ambition) and true contentment?

10. Start a list of all the things that every Christian receives once they come to the Father through faith in Jesus Christ.

    If we remember these things and keep our focus on them, how can this help contentment grow in our lives and free us from coveting?

11. Think about the times and seasons of your life when you felt the greatest levels of contentment and the lowest levels of coveting. What was it that led to contentment and freed you from coveting?

Celebrating and Being Celebrated

One of the ways we can keep from coveting is by thanking God for what we have and acknowledging that everything is a gift from him. As a group, lift up prayers of thanks for the things God has given to you. Use some of the prayer prompters below to get you started:

- Thank you for the place I live.
- Thank you for my family members.
- I give you praise for the friends you have placed in my life.
- Thank you for my job and how it provides for my needs (and wants).
- I give thanks for the vehicle I drive, the clothes I have, the furniture in my home.
- Other prayers of thanks ...

Loving and Being Loved

It is hard to be happy for others when we are coveting what they have and scheming ways to match it, surpass it, or even take it. But as we grow in contentment, we can be released from covetousness and we can admire, appreciate, and even affirm our neighbor.

Take time to humbly thank God for your neighbors. Ask him to give you a humble appreciation of the good things he has given them. Then make a point of telling a neighbor that you noticed a good thing they have and that you are happy for them. Really let them know that you rejoice with them!

Serving and Being Served

Th next time you have a few hours to spare and you're tempted to do a little recreational shopping, make a choice of courage. Sit down and read a Christian book, write out a prayer to God, listen to worship music, call or get together with a friend and talk about matters of importance, go for a jog, send an encouraging note, do some volunteer work around the church or in the community. Rather than acquire more stuff, invest in something that will lead to a richer life without filling up your closet or garage. If you want to take this idea a step further, give the money you would have spent at the shopping center to a ministry or someone in need.

Session One – Honor God as God
EXODUS 20:1–7

Question 1

The introduction includes a list of eight statements that point to eight different occupations (using their inside lingo and professional expressions). Here is the answer key:

1. Stockbroker
2. Computer programmer
3. Carpenter
4. Insurance salesperson
5. Dentist
6. Doctor, medical person
7. Bible professor, theologian
8. OB/GYN, pediatrician, delivery room nurse

Since every line of work has its own language and shorthand, we should not be surprised that the Bible (the book with the richest theology in all history) also has its own language. It is a divine book, breathed by the very breath of God (2 Timothy 3:16).

Sometimes the language of the Bible takes time to unpack, interpret, and understand. Understanding what it means to avoid idols and refuse to misuse God's name requires study and reflection. As a group, your discussion will help each of you go deeper in your understanding and application of these first three commandments.

Questions 2–3

The goal in these two questions is to look at both sides of these first three commandments. Every one of the Ten Commandments is like a two-sided coin, a call to *do* something and *not do* something.

For example, the first commandment is clear that we are to have no other gods before the one true God. On the one side, it means we are to scrutinize and remove those things that vie for first place in our heart. But it also means we are to honor God as God, lifting him up as the only one who deserves our praise. The first half of this equation could lead us to make sure a hobby we love does not dominate our life or pull us away from time in God's presence. In addition, we could take some of the time this pursuit has been occupying and spend it worshiping at the feet of Jesus, studying the Word, talking with our Savior in prayer.

Another example of this two-sided coin imagery involves how we use God's name. On the one side, we make a commitment to never use God's name as an expression of anger or frustration. Because his name is holy, we refrain from throwing it around as a curse or using it as profanity. But, on the other side, we regularly lift up God's name and his character for the sake of honoring him and letting the world know how good he is.

Questions 4–6

We are called to honor God as God and live gripped by his greatness, love, and wisdom. When we honor God as God, we discover what it is to live cleanly, to have peace of mind and heart. God says, "On the basis of what I did for you on the cross through Jesus Christ, if you repent of your sins and turn to me, I will forgive you and bring you into my family forever." The very first step toward obeying the first commandment is to believe God's assessment about our sinful condition and our need to repent of it. To obey this commandment we must first turn to Jesus Christ for salvation and invite him to make us right before God.

Another element of honoring God as God is finding out what he wants us to do with our lives and then following his plans and purpose. There is no such thing as honoring God as God without a commitment to obey him in everything. In order to really obey the first commandment, we must become extravagant risk-takers. Obeying the first commandment is not for the weak of heart. It means making tough choices. This could involve breaking off sinful relationships, speaking the truth when it is hard, and so on.

When we do this, God comes through and floods our life with approval, affirmation, and encouragement. Over time, as we honor God more completely, we experience the transforming work of the Holy Spirit. We find ourselves saying things like, "I didn't know it could feel so good to live this way; I'm discovering what it's like to live with a clean conscience; I'm tasting the goodness of integrity as I'm learning to be a truth-teller; I'm living with sexual purity; I have clean lips; I'm honoring you with my resources!" When we honor God as God, everything begins to change.

In addition, as we honor God as God, we begin to identify the idols we have set up in our heart. Before now, we haven't even noticed them. Psalm 115 and Isaiah 46 provide pictures of just how powerless and empty idols really are. As we honor God as God, idols stand out as pathetic substitutes and we are ready to look at the second commandment.

Questions 7–8

Throughout history people have set up idols (external objects or internal false images) in the hope of propping themselves up in times of need. The problem is that every idol fails us. They are powerless, empty, unable to offer the help we need. Only the one true God can do that.

All sorts of things can become idols. Even things that seem like good representations can become distractions that keep us from really looking to God. For instance, the crucifix has been a comforting image to millions and millions of Christians throughout the world. What Jesus did on the cross should never be forgotten and those who see a crucifix and remember Jesus' death on our behalf are on the right track. But those who fixate on the cross or a crucifix to the point of worship are wandering into the territory of idolatry. The only hope for this life and eternity is to trust in the sin-sacrifice that Jesus made for us on the cross. Any man-made object that points us to the cross can become reductionary if we stop with the object and forget the Savior who actually died on the cross and rose again for our salvation.

Many churches have baptismal fonts, communion tables, ornate pulpits, or other objects designed to help people worship

God as God. If they move us to do that ... great! If they take on special status and are seen as sacred ... be careful!

Mental images of God can also be reductionary and misleading. Some people carry a mental image of God as an angry judge pounding his gavel and shouting out a sentence of condemnation, "Guilty, guilty, guilty." Though not a physical picture or a man-made image, this nevertheless is a false image seared into the mind. These people need to meet God as their loving Father. They need to read the gospel of John and discover that God can be their ever-faithful friend. The truth of Scripture can shatter false mental images.

Bottom line, symbols, icons, and so on can help remind us of sacred events or our relationship to God, but they should never be objects of devotion in and of themselves.

Questions 9–11

People misuse the name of God in many ways. One obvious way is that they use it as profanity. We all need to guard our hearts and mouths when it comes to this kind of misuse of God's name.

Another misuse is speaking God's name as a form of leverage to get what we want from people or God. Children who try to buttress what they have said by declaring, "I swear to God," should be taught that this is dangerous. Even adults can use these words when they are trying to prove that what they are saying is true. Our word should be enough. We should not have to use God's name to pressure people to believe us ... especially when we are not telling the full truth, but still want to cover our tracks.

Session Two — Remember the Sabbath
EXODUS 20:8–11

Question 1

Anyone who has tried to go week after week with no rest, day off, or Sabbath pattern in their life knows that this puts every aspect of life at risk. This is why God calls us to be people who both work hard and rest well. The consequences of refusing to take a Sabbath can come in many shapes and forms. Here are just a handful of possible outcomes:

- *Physical:* Fatigue, aches, pains, sickness, and other ailments can consume our body.
- *Emotional:* Stress, anxiety, inability to sleep, and all kinds of tensions can creep into our life.
- *Relational:* Marriages can be beat up, even destroyed. Children can feel neglected and unloved. Friendships can become weak and fragmented. Every one of our relationships can be damaged when work takes over our life. Even work relationships can become strained because we are burning the candle at both ends.
- *Spiritual:* We can feel distant from God if we don't have time to feed on his Word or sit at his feet. We can also deal with guilt because we know we are not following the example our heavenly Father has set.
- *Others:* When work spins out of balance and consumes our life, everything is up for grabs. No part of our life is safe from the potential collateral damage.

In ancient Israel, the Sabbath was observed in the twenty-four-hour period from sundown Friday until sundown Saturday. After the resurrection of Jesus on the first day of the week, Christians began to gather to celebrate on Sunday (the first day). Some religious groups believe strongly that Sabbath must be observed on Saturday. Others hold that it must be on Sunday. But, the spirit of Sabbath seems to be primarily about the rhythm of six days of labor and one day of rest.

For pastors and church workers, Sunday and often Saturday have become work days. Does this make these people Sabbath breakers or consign them to a Sabbathless existence? No. These people might observe a Monday, Friday, or another day as their Sabbath. Doctors, nurses, firefighters, police, and many other occupations demand work on the weekend for the good of society. These people can take another day for their Sabbath. The real issue is not the exact day, but the commitment to observe Sabbath on a weekly basis as God has taught us.

Questions 2–3

We are to remember the Sabbath day and keep it holy ... sacred. John Calvin taught that the Sabbath day was to be a day very dissimilar from the other days of the week, one on which we refrain from our usual activities.

The Sabbath is to be a day when we do not work, either our regular work responsibilities or others. Some people click off from their regular job but simply dive into a list of twenty-seven items that need done around the house. The key is to set the work aside so that we can connect with God and each other in distinct ways. This call to cease and desist from our labors also carries over to our children and anyone who is in our home. Sabbath is so important that God does not want anyone to miss it.

In addition, this is a day of rest and refreshment. Just as our Father rested, we are to follow his example as loving children. We should discover things that replenish our soul and refresh our heart, mind, and body. These are things we should do on our Sabbath.

Questions 4–5

In our country, where the sky is the limit, we can work as much as we want. Even retired people can volunteer at church or in the community and still work seven days a week. If you work fifty hours, there is always somebody who will work sixty. If you work sixty hours, there is always somebody willing to work seventy. There is no end to what we can do. If we get sucked into the vortex of working more and more and more, we can start to believe that our work defines us, that it determines our value and rules our world.

In the session, you read a powerful quote from William Wilberforce, who committed to observe the Sabbath even when he had to force himself to do it. This rhythm sustained him when the pressures of life became almost unbearable and he lost vote after vote to overturn the slave trade he so hated. Some of his friends did not observe the Sabbath day as he did. In fact, two of his colleagues committed suicide. Out of that tragedy, Wilberforce wrote, "With peaceful Sundays, the strings would never have snapped as they did." He realized that the sustained tension they lived with eventually pushed them over the edge.

Questions 6–7

For more than a 150 hours a week we are subjected to a constant barrage of deceptive and often profane creeds, slogans, and jingles that take a toll on our value system. They beat us down, giving us fuzzy minds and causing us to lose perspective on who God is and who we are meant to be. Thus God says, "You need to come together regularly, rhythmically, so that you remember who I am and who you are." When we are in community, we hear fresh voices; we hear truth; we can connect with God and each other in ways that bring refreshment and peace that we can't get anywhere else.

We're prone to wander from the true course: to forget who God is, why we're here, who it is we're trying to please, who it is that gives our life meaning and value. God knows this proneness toward wandering and says, "At least every seven days, close the shop and come together and remember who I am. Remember what I can do in your life. Remember how much I care for you. Remember that I have a plan for your life, a grand purpose that will give your life meaning and satisfaction." God wants us to remember that his plan for us is more than just going through the motions of life.

Questions 8–9

We might not need to recalibrate every fifteen to twenty minutes, but the One who made us knows that once every week we need to unplug, step back, take our foot off the gas, and allow his Spirit to search our heart and help us regain our bearings. A full day of Sabbath rest is just what the Good Physician ordered. When we slow down, connect with God, intersect with other believers, and remember who we are, life gets back on course.

Questions 10–11

Some people have become so legalistic about the Sabbath that they do not see this as a day for fun, play, or refreshment. God is the most joyful being in the entire universe. He wants us to discover that this day can afford the chance to be refreshed in ways that the other six days of the week do not allow. We are wise to identify a few activities that really refresh and recharge us and incorporate these into our Sabbath day observance.

Session Three – Honor Your Parents
EXODUS 20:12; EPHESIANS 6:1–3

Question 1

The topic of this session can bring memories that are wonderful and precious as well as dredge up reminders of untold pain and sorrow. Take ample time as a group leader to pray for this session. Most groups will include participants who love their parents and have healthy, close relationships with them. There is also a good chance that some in your group have faced abuse or neglect at the hands of their parents. Ask God to give wisdom and sensitivity to group members in this discussion and to bring healing to broken hearts.

Questions 2–3

God is clear that long life is somehow connected to obeying the fifth commandment. The apostle Paul writes similarly. There is a tie (not an absolute promise, but a general truth) between our health and the years we live and our ability to honor and bless our parents.

In Ephesians the apostle Paul clarifies that obeying our parents is to be "in the Lord." The Bible does not call children to blindly obey parents no matter what they say. The implied understanding is that we obey parents who are operating under the Lord's leading. When parents call children to do something or live in a way that is consistent with the teaching of the Bible, we are to walk in obedience to their leadership.

Questions 4–6

Our lives go through seasons. But in every season this commandment to honor our parents holds true.

For the most part, younger children follow this commandment by obeying what their parents teach even when they don't understand why. As we move into adolescence and young adulthood, simple obedience becomes more about collaborating with parents. Obedience in this season of life is about an enduring respect: in our tone, attitude, and actions. It is also about cooperation, showing honor rather than constantly resisting and pushing back. As adults, we can continue to honor our parents by treasuring them. This is a season when respect, words of thanks, and actions of blessing continue the legacy of honor that parents deserve.

Questions 7–9

My guess is that a sizeable number of people who think about the fifth commandment fight back the urge to cry out, "How can I honor parents who were not honorable? Must I honor people who didn't treat me with dignity?" Through the years, when I have preached on this topic, letters always start pouring in. People tell me things like, "The very idea of honoring my father and mother is a painful concept for me to grasp because my father sexually abused me as a child and my mother looked the other way and chose to do nothing. How could I possibly honor my parents? Do you really believe this commandment applies to me?"

So many adults can tell stories of parents who were alcoholics, workaholics, abusive, neglectful, cold, and uncaring. Many have lived with parents who have caused deep pain and disappointment. Is God demanding that these people put on a happy face and pretend there is no pain? Is God demanding that hurting people simply submerge their highly charged feelings and blindly go about the duty of honoring the very people who have wronged and wounded them? Will God settle for inauthentic honor?

He will not.

He does not want or expect false and hollow honor. What he does ask is that we deal with our pain, hurt, and brokenness. God knows that ignoring our pain and burying our past will not lead to things going well with us or long life. Indeed, such wounds can become a cancer in our soul and even our body. God calls us to address the past so we can live for him in the future.

Questions 10–11

What good news! No matter how absent or even hurtful an earthly parent might have been, God is a perfect heavenly Father. Those who have always longed for a parent who would bless them, protect them, and love them can find all of this and more in the tender arms of God. For many people, the first step toward healing in their relationship with earthly parents is to devote time and energy to build up their relationship with the heavenly Father.

Session Four — Protect and Honor Life
EXODUS 20:13–14; MATTHEW 5:21–30

Question 1

Some people might be quick to say, "Our society already does endorse and accept both murder and adultery as normal." Though in some ways there is a growing acceptance of behaviors (both physical and spiritual) that God would call murderous and adulterous, thankfully, there is not a wholesale embrace of these practices.

As a group, imagine what culture and society would really be like if everyone cast off all restraint and had no value for life. This picture will help us see why God has placed these boundaries on his children. This is not a sign of a limiting, mean-spirited deity who is trying to ruin our fun. On the contrary, it is a sign that God loves his children and wants the best for us.

Questions 2–3

In Matthew 5:21–30 Jesus takes the sixth and seventh commandments and unpacks them. For those who declare with pride, "Hey, I have never killed anyone or taken someone else's spouse," Jesus says, "Let's look a little deeper at these commandments and the spirit of what they say." Jesus is clear that anger is murder's twin sister. He also wants us to know that lust is the launchpad for adultery. Even if we have not murdered someone or committed adultery, there is a good chance we have dealt with anger, harsh words, and lust.

Questions 4–5

Underneath the sixth commandment is an implicit concern for protecting people from any physical violence, not just murder. Many places in Scripture, God shows his disdain for people striking each other. Sadly, I'm afraid that we as a society are becoming accustomed to interpersonal violence instead of being radically revolted by it. We tune in to television shows and watch movies knowing in advance by the teasers that violence and bloodshed will be central to the story. As followers of the Prince of Peace we should pause to ask if these are the right kind of images to record in the database of our heart.

Questions 6–7

Jesus says that no one has the right to murder a person's reputation, character, or self-esteem. People come to me years after they've left home, and they can tell me word for word the kinds of bullets that came out of their parents' mouths. They say to me, with their heads hung low, "My parents called me 'stupid.' They called me 'ugly 'or 'useless.' They told me over and over again I was a jerk and I'd never amount to anything." When I listen to these people, I really get the impression that when their parents talked to them that way, a small part of them died.

And this problem is not a one-way street. Sometimes children say terrible things to parents, and part of the parent dies. Or a spouse launches verbal missiles at the one they should be protecting and blessing. Verbal violence (including racial slurs, ethnic slaps, and sexual shots) happens in the home, at work, at school—everywhere. Every time a human being lashes out with their tongue, damaging someone's self-esteem or character or reputation, a small murder occurs.

Questions 8–9

It is important to remember that our sexuality is a God-designed gift. As difficult as it may be for us to believe, our holy, righteous, completely pure God delights in the tender, caring sexual expressions of love that occur between a husband and wife. He wrote in his Word that the marriage bed is to be undefiled. That simply means that within the right context—within the biblically defined parameters of a man and a woman in a marriage—there should be no shame in the expression of our sexuality. In Hebrews 13:4 and 1 Corinthians 7:3–5, God specifically instructs husbands and wives to be responsive to each other's sexual needs. In Proverbs 5:15–19, God calls people to celebrate sexual expression within the marriage relationship. No matter how much the world tries to destroy and pervert sexuality, it is still a good gift from God when expressed within biblical boundaries.

Questions 10–11

Our sexual urges are powerful, our society's values are permissive, and our marriages are becoming increasingly difficult. The question now is, how will any of us be able to stay faithful to our spouses? What will it take to obey the seventh commandment for the rest of our lives?

First and foremost, it will take a vital relationship with Jesus Christ. When you're a fully devoted follower of Jesus Christ you build your first and best line of defense.

A *second* key to obeying the seventh commandment is a sober-minded view of your own sexuality. Matthew 10:16 says we should be wise as serpents but gentle as doves. We need to be wary of the early warning signals of sexual temptation. We should take appropriate measures to reduce the possibility of being in the wrong place at the wrong time in the wrong condition with the wrong person.

The *third* key for being able to obey the seventh commandment over the long haul is to develop a discerning attitude toward our permissive society. It is time for Christians to say, "Enough is enough. I will no longer let certain forms of input have access to my mind. Certain books, magazines, television shows, and movies are off-limits. Spiritual surgery is going to be performed for the sake of spiritual purity." Whenever we cut off a particular kind of input or activity or experience for the purpose of sexual purity, God honors it.

A *fourth* key to help us keep the seventh commandment is to develop a determination to enrich our own marriage. If a married couple is carefully nurturing, serving, enriching, inspiring, and romancing one another, the odds of infidelity are greatly, greatly reduced.

Session Five – The Essential Place of Honesty
EXODUS 20:15–16

Question 1

This session of the Ten Commandments discussion guide deals with some very personal topics around the theme of honesty. As leader, be sure to remind group members not to use names of people or examples that will identify someone. In the process of group sharing, you do not want to create an environment for gossip.

Questions 2–3

God calls us to be honest in our relationships for his glory and for our good. He knows that dishonesty in our words or actions (through stealing) destroys community, families, marriages, friendships, and every relationship we have. Again, God gives these commandments not to ruin our fun but to give us healthy relationships and the kind of intimacy with people that our heart desires.

Questions 4–5

The Bible does not forbid acquiring personal property nor does it teach that things are bad in and of themselves. It simply says there's an acceptable and unacceptable way to acquire property. The first and most obvious way to acquire things is through diligent labor. Work hard, receive remuneration, and then buy the things you need. As you cooperate with God's plan for acquiring personal property in this fashion, you will also, as a side benefit, develop self-respect, self-esteem, and confidence.

A second biblically acceptable way of acquiring personal property is through wise trading or investing. In Matthew 25 Jesus tells a story of a man with five talents who traded and invested them in such a way that they doubled. Jesus commended him for this.

A third God-honoring means of acquiring resources is through believing prayer. From time to time, God intervenes and provides certain personal property items as a gift from his gracious hand. Almost all of us could tell a story about a time when we prayed because we had a need and God supplied it.

Questions 6–7

The eighth commandment forbids seizure, deception, and defrauding others. We defraud someone when we withhold what is rightfully due them. God wants his children to function with honesty in all of our relationships and personal dealings. This means we need to scrutinize our heart, our motives, our behaviors. If we see areas where we are stealing through blatant and dishonest actions or through subtle behaviors, we can blow the whistle on ourselves. We can confess this to God and, if need be, to others.

Questions 8–10

There are countless examples of how we can be tempted to lie or deceive. Here are a few:

- "My speedometer must have malfunctioned, Officer."
- "I didn't see the sign."
- "I would've finished this assignment, but you wouldn't believe what happened."
- Parents lie when they write a sick note for a child who was not really sick.
- Secretaries lie when they answer the phone and say the boss is out when he really isn't. Parents likewise ask their kids to lie about their whereabouts and teach them wrong behavior in the process.
- We call in sick to work some days and then have a "miraculous healing" that allows us to go shopping or do other things.
- Someone invites us to serve in some way and we say, "I'll be there." In our spirit, we know we have no intention of going. But for convenience sake, we say we will.

Session Six — Restrain Material Desires
EXODUS 20:17; COLOSSIANS 3:1–3

Question 1

As a student of human nature, I'm always fascinated by the diversity of objects that people covet. I knew a man whose whole world revolved around the dream of owning a sailboat. That desire eclipsed every other concern in his life.

I knew a young couple who had plans for a house they were going to build someday. That dream house was the driving force in their lives. They both worked and seldom relaxed or played because of their all-consuming passion to build their dream house. Their conversations tended to circle back to "the house." Their limited free time was spent paging through magazines for more creative ideas about their home. Their budget and spending patterns were focused on their goal; not even God's work could tempt them to divert a dollar away from attaining it.

I have known others who were driven to expand their wardrobe, increase their stamp collection, widen their travel itineraries, enlarge their investment portfolio, build a collection of movies, own all the best toys, and so much more. Instead of their primary loyalty being toward God it was diverted toward the acquisition of a particular commodity or object.

In the marketplace, management teams have learned how to dangle attractive inducements in front of salespeople: Caribbean vacations, luxury golf getaways, and so on. The message is clear: fix your gaze on these premiums; pin your hopes on these rewards; and let your desire for them grow until it drives you to outsell, outhustle, and outperform your colleagues.

I'm not suggesting that all incentive programs are ill advised. I'm simply going on record as saying that if salespeople aren't careful, they're going to find themselves coveting the prize so acutely that they will neglect their spouse, their children, their health, their church, and their God in order to win a monetary prize.

The first commandment teaches that whatever we fix our gaze on and pursue with our whole heart (other than God) will wind up disappointing us someday. If a young couple finally builds their dream home, they'll soon discover that the paint fades and the carpet wears and the house doesn't satisfy the soul.

They might even discover that after all the years of obsession over building a house they forgot to build a marriage.

Coveting is like the proverbial carrot on the stick. It drives us to work, acquire, and gather ... but it never satisfies. It is like salt water to a person dying of thirst.

Questions 2–3

The Bible deals with money, finances, covetousness, and contentment over and over again, from the Old Testament to the New. It is one of the central spiritual topics in Scripture. God gives so many stern warnings because he knows the seductive power of money and the human tendency to want what others have. He wants us to know that the enemy of our soul is quick to use material goods as a hook to catch us and pull us away from what matters most.

Questions 4–5

The first commandment and the tenth commandment are God's attempt to help us realize that a living and growing relationship with God is what we need the most in the final analysis. No material substitute will do. Whatever else we fix our gaze on will disappoint us and leave us alienated, confused, and alone. And the sooner we reach that conclusion, the more heartbreak we will save ourselves from.

If we are going to be free to love God and released from the lure of worldly goods, we need to learn how to admire and appreciate what others have but not covet and desire it. There is a fine distinction here. Take time as a group to identify what it looks like when we admire and appreciate in a way that honors God. Also articulate what it looks like when we slip into the sin of coveting.

When we think of a person murdering another person, we are sure that God's heart breaks. When adultery destroys a marriage and devastates children, we can be confident the heart of God grieves. But what about coveting? If we are going to battle this sin, we need to see it the way God does. Coveting is a form of idolatry. It seduces us and draws us away from the one true God, causing us to live with a divided heart. It allows stuff to slip in with sinister stealth and climb onto the throne of our heart.

If you read the Old Testament you will discover that idolatry was one of the worst sins of God's people. God takes it very seriously.

Questions 6–7

Have you ever seen film of salmon swimming upstream? These fish struggle, strain, and fight their way against the current. This is what it is like to live in modern culture and seek to resist the marketing of greed and selfishness. Much of our modern economy and society is based on a system of living that expects us to spend much of our time thinking about stuff, earning money so we can purchase more stuff, buying things, taking care of our storehouses of things, insuring our toys, and basing our sense of self-worth on the quantity and quality of our stuff.

When we learn to identify the errant nature of this kind of living, we can fight back. We can put on filters that will keep us from getting sucked into any and every new marketing scheme that Madison Avenue dreams up.

Questions 9–11

Jesus teaches that having plenty of material resources doesn't necessarily give a man or a woman a plentiful spirit. We all know of people who are affluent with respect to material resources but who have bankrupt lives, relationships, and hearts.

True contentment frees us from covetousness. When our relationship with God is our central and consuming passion, gathering things takes its rightful place in our life and seems far less important. When we are thankful for what we have and not impassioned to acquire more, we can actually enjoy our possessions as a good gift from the hand of a loving Father. When we are released from the sin of coveting, we can admire and appreciate what our neighbor has and let them know that we truly rejoice with them and for them.

We value your thoughts about what you've just read.
Please share them with us. You'll find contact information
in the back of this book.

WILLOW
Willow Creek Resources

Willow Creek Association
Vision, Training, Resources for Prevailing Churches

This resource was created to serve you and to help you build a local church that prevails. It is just one of many ministry tools published by the Willow Creek Association.

The Willow Creek Association (WCA) was created in 1992 to serve a rapidly growing number of churches from across the denominational spectrum that are committed to helping unchurched people become fully devoted followers of Christ. Membership in the WCA now numbers over 12,000 Member Churches worldwide from more than ninety denominations.

The Willow Creek Association links like-minded Christian leaders with each other and with strategic vision, training and resources in order to help them build prevailing churches designed to reach their redemptive potential.

For specific information about WCA conferences, resources, membership and other ministry services contact:

Willow Creek Association
P.O. Box 3188
Barrington, IL 60011-3188
Phone: 847.570.9812
Fax: 847.765.5046
www.willowcreek.com

Just Walk Across the Room Curriculum Kit

Simple Steps Pointing People to Faith

Bill Hybels with *Ashley Wiersma*

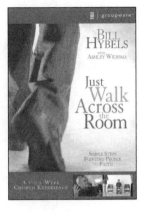

In *Just Walk Across the Room*, Bill Hybels brings personal evangelism into the twenty-first century with a natural and empowering approach modeled after Jesus himself. When Christ "walked" clear across the cosmos more than 2,000 years ago, he had no forced formulas and no memorized script; rather, he came armed only with an offer of redemption for people like us, many of whom were neck-deep in pain of their own making.

This dynamic four-week experience is designed to equip and inspire your entire church to participate in that same pattern of grace-giving by taking simple walks across rooms—leaving your circles of comfort and extending hands of care, compassion, and inclusiveness to people who might need a touch of God's love today.

Expanding on the principles set forth in Hybels' book of the same name, *Just Walk Across the Room* consists of three integrated components:

- Sermons, an implementation guide, and church promotional materials provided on CD-ROM to address the church as a whole
- Small group DVD and a participant's guide to enable people to work through the material in small, connected circles of community
- The book *Just Walk Across the Room* to allow participants to think through the concepts individually

Mixed Media Set: 978-0-310-27172-7

Pick up a copy at your favorite bookstore!

When the Game Is Over,
It All Goes Back in the Box DVD

Six Sessions on Living Life in the Light of Eternity

John Ortberg with *Stephen* and
Amanda Sorenson

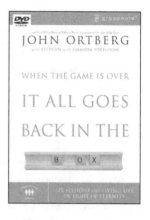

Using his humor and his genius for storytelling,
John Ortberg helps you focus on the real rules
of the game of life and how to set your priorities.
*When the Game Is Over, It All Goes Back in the
Box DVD* and participant's guide help explain
how, left to our own devices, we tend to seek out
worldly things, mistakenly thinking they will bring
us fulfillment. But everything on Earth belongs to
God. Everything we "own" is just on loan. And what
pleases God is often 180 degrees from what we may think is important.

In the six sessions you will learn how to:

- Live passionately and boldly
- Learn how to be active players in the game that pleases God
- Find your true mission and offer your best
- Fill each square on the board with what matters most
- Seek the richness of being instead of the richness of having

You can't beat the house, notes Ortberg. We're playing our game of life
on a giant board called a calendar. Time will always run out, so it's a good
thing to live a life that delights your Creator. When everything goes back in
the box, you'll have made what is temporary a servant to what is eternal, and
you'll leave this life knowing you've achieved the only victory that matters.

This DVD includes a 32-page leader's guide and is designed to be used
with the *When the Game Is Over, It All Goes Back in the Box* participant's
guide, which is available separately.

DVD-ROM: 978-0-310-28247-1
Participant's Guide: 978-0-310-28246-4

Pick up a copy at your favorite bookstore!

The Case for Christ DVD

A Six-Session Investigation of the Evidence for Jesus

Lee Strobel and *Garry Poole*

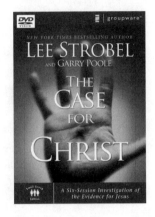

Is there credible evidence that Jesus of Nazareth really is the Son of God?

Retracing his own spiritual journey from atheism to faith, Lee Strobel, former legal editor of the *Chicago Tribune*, cross-examines several experts with doctorates from schools like Cambridge, Princeton, and Brandeis who are recognized authorities in their own fields.

Strobel challenges them with questions like:

- How reliable is the New Testament?
- Does evidence for Jesus exist outside the Bible?
- Is there any reason to believe the resurrection was an actual event?

Strobel's tough, point-blank questions make this six-session video study a captivating, fast-paced experience. But it's not fiction. It's a riveting quest for the truth about history's most compelling figure.

The six sessions include:

1. The Investigation of a Lifetime
2. Eyewitness Evidence
3. Evidence Outside the Bible
4. Analyzing Jesus
5. Evidence for the Resurrection
6. Reaching the Verdict

6 sessions; 1 DVD with leader's guide, 80 minutes (approximate).
The Case for Christ participant's guide is available separately.

DVD-ROM: 978-0-310-28280-8
Participant's Guide: 978-0-310-28282-2

Pick up a copy at your favorite bookstore!

ZONDERVAN®
.com

The Case for a Creator DVD

A Six-Session Investigation of the Scientific Evidence That Points toward God

Lee Strobel and *Garry Poole*

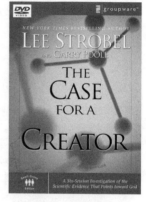

Former journalist and skeptic Lee Strobel has discovered something very interesting about science. Far from being the enemy of faith, science may now provide a solid foundation for believing in God.

Has science finally discovered God? Certainly new discoveries in such scientific disciplines as cosmology, cellular biology, astronomy, physics and DNA research are pointing to the incredible complexity of our universe, a complexity best explained by the existence of a Creator.

Written by Lee Strobel and Garry Poole, this six-session, 80-minute DVD curriculum comes with a companion participant's guide along with a leader's guide. The kit is based on Strobel's book and documentary *The Case for a Creator* and invites participants to encounter a diverse and impressive body of new scientific research that supports the belief in God. Weighty and complex evidence is delivered in a compelling conversational style.

The six sessions include:

1. Science and God
2. Doubts about Darwinism
3. The Evidence of Cosmology
4. The Fine-tuning of the Universe
5. The Evidence of Biochemistry
6. DNA and the Origin of Life

The Case for a Creator participant's guide is available separately.

DVD-ROM: 978-0-310-28283-9
Participant's Guide: 978-0-310-28285-3

Pick up a copy at your favorite bookstore!

ZONDERVAN®
.com

Share Your Thoughts

With the Author: Your comments will be forwarded to
the author when you send them to *zauthor@zondervan.com*.

With Zondervan: Submit your review of this book
by writing to *zreview@zondervan.com*.

Free Online Resources at
www.zondervan.com

Zondervan AuthorTracker: Be notified whenever your favorite
authors publish new books, go on tour, or post an update
about what's happening in their lives at www.zondervan.com/
authortracker.

Daily Bible Verses and Devotions: Enrich your life with daily
Bible verses or devotions that help you start every morning
focused on God. Visit www.zondervan.com/newsletters.

Free Email Publications: Sign up for newsletters on Christian
living, academic resources, church ministry, fiction, children's
resources, and more. Visit www.zondervan.com/newsletters.

Zondervan Bible Search: Find and compare Bible passages in
a variety of translations at www.zondervanbiblesearch.com.

Other Benefits: Register yourself to receive online benefits
like coupons and special offers, or to participate in research.

ZONDERVAN®

ZONDERVAN.com/
AUTHORTRACKER
follow your favorite authors